# Prospering Against Adversity

with Patience and Forgiveness

**Gwendolyn Singleterry**

# Prospering Against Adversity

## with Patience and Forgiveness

### Gwendolyn Singleterry

Detroit, MI, USA

Prospering Against Adversity with Patience and Forgiveness
Copyright © 2016 Gwendolyn Singleterry

All scripture quotations, unless otherwise indicated, are taken from the HOLY BIBLE, KING JAMES VERSION and are marked (KJV).

All rights reserved. No part of this publication may be reproduced, stored in a retrieval system, or transmitted in any form or by any means – electronic, mechanical, photocopy, recording, or any other – except for brief quotations in printed reviews, without the prior permission of the publisher.

NOTE: The author acknowledges that correctly written English capitalizes all proper nouns. However, throughout this work all references to the person of satan are not capitalized as a display of Christ's triumph over him.

*Priority*ONE Publications
P. O. Box 34722 • Detroit, MI 48234 USA
E-mail: info@priorityonebooks.com
URL: http://www.priorityonebooks.com

ISBN 13: 978-1-933972-46-6
ISBN 10:    1-933972-46-7

*Editing by Sheraee Crawford and Daphyene Hatcher*
*Cover and Interior design by PriorityONE Publications*
*Photoshoot by J. Michael Collins*

Printed in the United States of America

# Dedication

I dedicate this book to my daughter, Jonique Rance. There is no question that you have my heart – forever.

To my sister, Bernice Ellis. I love you.

To my deceased mother, Annie McKibbens. I thank God for you every day. God uses your words often to guide me in the way I should go. I miss you so much.

To all my angels. May you learn from my mistakes and grow in the knowledge of our Lord Jesus Christ.

Gwendolyn

# Scriptural Foundation

*My brethren,*
*count it all joy when ye fall into divers temptations;*
*Knowing this, that the trying of your faith worketh patience.*
*But let patience have her perfect work,*
*that ye may be perfect and entire, wanting nothing.*
James 1:2-4 KJV

*Honor for*

*Gwendolyn Singleterry*

I was born the year my aunt graduated from high school. She says that's how she remembers how many years she has been out of high school. My mother had five kids and my aunt took each of us under her wing. She is the best sister that my mother could have been blessed with. From the day each one of us was born, she was there as we grew up. When Christmas came, our living room looked like a store with toys and clothes.

My aunt is a sophisticated lady that knows how to dress and how to carry herself as a woman when she walks out the door. Wherever she goes, heads turn. When she walks into church you see a Proverbs 31:25 woman. "Strength and honor are clothing; and she shall rejoice in time to come." Not only does my aunt dress, but she has always dressed her daughter, nieces and nephews. She has even dressed the children of strangers.

Proverbs 31:26 says, "She opens her mouth with wisdom; and in her tongue is the law of kindness." My aunt speaks with wisdom and tells you the truth whether you like it or not, she speaks what is on her mind.

Proverbs 31:30 says, "Favour is deceitful, and beauty is vain; but a woman that fears the Lord, she shall be praised." My aunt truly fears the Lord; she will minister and say get your life together. My aunt is a woman that believes in prayer. When the word of God says pray without ceasing, she will pray until she reaches heaven. She believes in praying for family and is the one that brings the family together. She believes in family reunion; she is truly a prayer warrior.

Proverbs 28:27 says, "He that gives unto the poor shall not lack." My Aunt will never be without because she believes in giving with a loving heart. She will give her last.

Matthew 5:16 says "Let your light so shine before men, that they may see your good works, and glorify your Father which is in heaven." My aunt is that light you see whether she is on the mountain or even when she is in the valley - the light is still shining.

My aunt will praise and dance before the Lord. When you see my Aunt, you have seen that Proverbs 31:10 woman, "who can find a virtuous woman? For her price is far above rubies."

Cynthia Walker

This is the life of Auntie Gwen seen in the eyes of her niece, Lovise Ellis McKinney. From the beginning of my life, Aunt Gwen had a part in who I am. Before she knew my mother was having a girl, she saw this name, and felt lead in her Spirit to ask my mother to name me Lovise. And with this name I have been set apart from others.

Aunt Gwen is a woman of God who hears and obeys the voice of the Holy Spirit. She's one who if you don't want to see what you are believing will come to pass, then don't ask Aunt Gwen to pray because even when you get weary, Aunt Gwen still holds onto the promises of God. For example, I asked Aunt Gwen to pray for God to open the door for my husband and I to purchase our first home. Well, during this time the thief rose up against my husband, but this didn't stop Aunt Gwen. She kept praying knowing God had revealed it was our time to purchase a home. In the end, we did move into our brand new home – and to God be the glory!

Aunt Gwen is a woman who not only moves in the Spirit, but the natural. If Aunt Gwen has a need and she hears from the Holy Spirit, she does not look at her need or circumstance because she walks by faith knowing that the need will be met. She's truly a giver.

Not only has she been a blessing to my family, but to our whole family and to countless friends as well. It's using her gift to bake cakes or cook, and man can she cook.

I truly thank God for Aunt Gwen, she's more than an Aunt to me; she's more than a giver, she's God sent.

Sincerely,
Lovise McKinney

Gwendolyn Singleterry is not a Christian that lives life as a spectator sport standing on the sidelines crying and licking her wounds; but rather is a progressive participant that has endured the test of time as spoken in James 1:1-18 (The Message Bible). I can attest to that because I have known her for almost ten years and in those years despite the flesh's natural desire to flee at the first sign of adversity. As a believer she has conquered many of life's challenges through the power of prayer, patience, and faith. Be it lack of finances, family turbulence or making a decision on the direction of her career, patience has taught her to wait on the Lord.

In doing so in the true spirit of God to which wisdom is freely given and patience is learned, Gwendolyn Singleterry shares her knowledge of patience to those that inquire. God has equipped her through the Holy Spirit to utilize her ministry of patience to assist others in navigating the course of life. She believes that "iron sharpens iron" (Proverbs 27:17 KJV) for she has guided me through some of the most troubling of times by taking me to the word of God and sharing similar experiences with me.

It is not by accident that Gwendolyn Singleterry is still on this earth and is enjoying the season of winter. I truly believe that God placed her here to minister to the less seasoned in order to – like her, be able to receive the manifested blessings of God and continue to press our way to the finish line armed with patience.

Daphyene Hatcher

Gwen Singleterry is a vibrant woman of God who I have the honor of knowing as Mama Gwen. Not only does she drive my favorite car, wear some of the sharpest clothes, always has a jazzy hairstyle, and makes some of the best homemade pound cakes I have ever eaten, but most importantly, she loves with the love of the Father. You see, behind all of the things I mentioned above, she is a worshipping warrior who stands upon the Word of God, and speaks the truth unashamedly and unapologetically. She always has a word of encouragement to share, a hug to give, and a prayer waiting in the wings for whatever need may arise. She is an intercessor who will call you first thing in the morning to say, "Angel, the Lord put you on my heart this morning and He wants you to know..." When our conversations begin like that, before you know it we are on the phone praying for over an hour, for everything and everyone.

I will never forget the first time I met Mama Gwen; it was at 6:00 a.m. prayer, and I remember her walking in, sitting down, and just silently waiting. I was observing her as she was observing the environment, and as prayer began, she lifted her arms in worship, and it was as if no one else was there besides her and God. I was so intrigued as a babe in Christ, and in that moment, I knew that I wanted to be able to do that; just tune everything out that was going on around me, and be as one with the Father.

After prayer, I didn't have an opportunity to speak to her as we were all headed to the 8:00 a.m. service. In the main entrance, as worship began, here came Mama Gwen up at the altar with tambourine in hand, taking off her shoes, and praising, worshipping, and dancing before her God not giving anything or anyone else another thought. I remember saying to myself, "wow, I will do that one day."

After service, I walked up to her, introduced myself, and told her that I admired her courage, and that I saw passion in her worship that I wanted to carry one day. Her words to me were, "Angel, when you have gone through tough times, sometimes all you can do is worship. You already have it inside of you and in time it will come forth at an even greater level than you think is possible because it is not about us, but it is all about Him." In that moment I knew there was an authenticity and wisdom in the words she spoke to me from a place of humility. I took those words and held on to them and years later, as a worshipper, I still carry those words in my spirit today.

Mama Gwen sees others through the eyes of the Father, and with love of the Father. She does not need to be seen or heard; she is not concerned about position or title or a role, or even being acknowledged. She is happy just staying in the background, interceding, worshipping, serving, giving, and loving people, walking in obedience, while being about the Father's business. She operates in a Wisdom and Grace that serves as an example to those she comes in contact with. She brings the light of hope and the truth of the Word in any situation. She is the daughter of the King, the sister to all, and the mother to many. I thank God for Mama Gwen, and I count it an honor and a privilege to know her, and serve with her in the body of Christ for such a time as this.

Autumn Horvath

I met Ms. Gwen when I was 19 years old (over 30 years ago). Being the evangelist that she is, she was very kind to me in inviting me to her church and always telling me about the Lord. She never badgered me, but ministered to me through love (and her cooking). When I did decide to attend her church, I went on Father's Day, 1980 and got baptized in Jesus' name that same Sunday. From that point on she took me under her wing and showed me through love what a "classy, jazzy" woman of God should be and always giving me words of encouragement and words of wisdom. Her style, her elegance, but most of all, her walk with the Lord is what influenced me to live holy. Even when she moved away from Michigan and returned – somehow we made contact again.

I always brag about Ms. Gwen to my friends that I want to be like her when I get big. Her style, her relationship with the Lord, how she still works full-time even at her graceful stage of life, I admire her more than she may know.

In my conclusion, besides God, I owe thanks to Ms. Gwen for leading me to the Lord through love. Thank you, Ms. Gwen for being obedient to your evangelistic call and being the awesome example of the Godly woman that you are.

Sincerely,<br>Wilma Laster

Gwendolyn Singleterry is one of the kindest, most generous persons I have ever known. I have known Gwen all of my life (63 years) because she is my godmother. From the time I was born she has been giving to me. My mother had four children and no husband and Gwen would always help her out buying my Easter outfits and buying me Christmas presents. Gwen kept my hair looking good all of my childhood and teen years. When I was in college and had my daughter, Gwen did not judge me, but would even buy her clothes. She treated me the same in spite of my mistake and encouraged me.

Gwen is and has always been an eloquent dresser. She inspired me to look nice at all times and especially going to church. Ms. Singleterry is an excellent cook that doesn't mind sharing her knowledge and recipes with others. Ms. Gwen often prepares big meals for her family and friends. She does not mind cooking for others when they are in need.

And last, but not least Gwen is a pillar of faith. She has an awesome faith in God that guides every step in her life. She is a great prayer warrior for her friends and family. Because of her strong faith and godly counsel, my faith has grown tremendously in God. Gwen is such a caring and trusting (sometimes too kind and trusting) person. She would give you the shirt off her back if you needed it.

I will end my letter just by mentioning how Gwen cared for her mother until she passed away. Gwen left her home in another state to go home and take care of her mother. She took excellent care of her mother until the day she died. Gwen has an unconditional selfless love for people. I thank God that He gave me Ms. Gwendolyn Holmes Singleterry for a godmother.

Sincerely Yours,<br>Beverly Rushin

# Foreword

It's not often that one finds God-fearing ingenuity, entrepreneurial spirit, and humility in the same person. Yet, Gwendolyn Singleterry is such an individual. As a child, the desire to demonstrate love for her mother fueled the inquisitive and resourceful nature that caused her to establish her own business, at the tender age of twelve. As an adult she chose to learn from her mistakes, and the mistakes of others, all while learning that God's faithfulness and love are to be embraced with obedience and trust.

Believers often joke about not asking for patience because, as the King James Version of Romans 5:3 says, "tribulation worketh patience." I can only smile when I think of that verse as I read the accounts from Gwendolyn Singleterry's life. She is more than just a testament to the reality that trouble comes to every life. She demonstrates that even when some of that trouble is self-inflicted, through the accidental or malicious acts of others, or simply because of the fallen nature of mankind, it is better to learn, grow, and mature through it, instead of always fearing or attempting to avoid it.

Though Gwendolyn shares many troubling, yet intriguing moments from her life, this book is more than a memoir with colorful pictures of days gone by. It is a challenge to any reader who would dare consider how life's perilous moments are actually lessons to be learned. When those lessons teach us the value of trusting God, no matter how horrific life becomes, we would do well to remember and take notes. By documenting her own travels through life, and the lessons of patience and forgiveness she learned from them, she has left a legacy of God's faithfulness for her family and ours. By asking questions at the end of each chapter, Gwendolyn invites the reader to begin a personal journey of self-discovery that causes one's own memories to come flooding in. When that happens, don't hesitate to write them down in the spaces provided.

Too often we assume that we will remember the stories of how we perceived life as children or by God's grace, narrowly escaped our own perils; not to mention the stories our parents and grandparents may have told us over the years. Yet, life's unpredictability begs to differ. It is important for us to record every memory, along with its lessons, as precious treasure to be discovered by generations to come. Kudos to Gwendolyn Singleterry for taking the journey and inviting us to come along.

Christina Dixon
*Book Coach*

# Table of Contents

Dedication & Scriptural Foundation ............................................. 5

Honor for Gwendolyn Singleterry................................................. 7

Foreword ........................................................................................ 17

Table of Contents.......................................................................... 19

Introduction .................................................................................. 21

Chapter 1 – Childhood ................................................................. 23

Chapter 2 – Talent ........................................................................ 29

Chapter 3 – Witchcraft ................................................................. 39

Chapter 4 – The Challenges of Adulthood ................................. 45

Chapter 5 – Becoming a Worshipper ......................................... 59

Chapter 6 – Life Moves You Around........................................... 65

Chapter 8 – Scripture to Stand On ............................................. 75

Photo Album.................................................................................. 79

Encouraging Words to Live By..................................................... 83

About the Author .......................................................................... 89

# Introduction

Patience is something I never had. Like a flower that grows between cracks in cement, patience struggled to grow in my life. When God spoke to me on February 15, 2014, and told me to write a book on patience, I remembered how my mother often told me, "Gwen, get some patience."

Since then, I have learned that patience is the art of waiting, the capacity to accept or tolerate delay, trouble, or suffering without getting angry. In other words, waiting on God's instruction which develops obedience. And in my waiting it also developed my patience. I found that patience allowed me to hear God's voice giving instructions which led me to become obedient. Who knew that by developing patience a new creature was being created, who now, God could trust to be immediately obedient to His word? God knows how to strengthen you in your weak areas. I have learned that patience is needed as you walk this walk with God.

2015 marked 56 years as a licensed cosmetologist and I am still working. No one, but God, has kept me; and I can still outwork some of the younger beauticians. My work is fast and good and all the credit goes to my God.

Over the last 4 years, business decreased, but I've learned how to be patient and trust God. I don't wait to get customers and then praise Him. I thank Him and praise Him as if I have already received them. When my bills are due, I give them to God because I am a prayer warrior.

Angels, God tests us because He wants us to grow so He can trust us in small matters before He leads us to greater work and service for Him. James 1:4 says, "Let patience have her perfect work in you and you may be perfect and entire, wanting nothing." That is why I've been asking God to increase my faith and develop patience in me.

Yes, Romans 5:3 teaches us that tribulation works patience and I suppose, if we could get patience without it, we would all like to avoid it. Lord knows I didn't want my share of it. But there is no escaping the trouble that comes with living. So, I decided that I might as well cooperate with God; especially since there is no counsel against Him (Proverbs 21:30).

# Chapter 1 – Childhood

**Lesson: Whether or not they were happy, write down all your childhood memories. It's family history.**

It was the early 40's; I was 8-years-old and my sister was 7-years-old. My great aunt Mattie kept my sister and me when we came home from school. One day she told my mother that she was tired of keeping us. My mother sat the two of us in a chair and told us that Great Aunt Mattie did not want to keep us anymore and that there was no one else to keep us. "You're going to have to keep yourselves," she said. She gave me a key and instructed us that no other children were allowed to come to play with us while she was not home; except one little girl named Sally Lois. My mother felt comfortable with Sally Lois and the way her parents were raising her. With all the things that could have happened to us with no adult supervision, I'm glad that my sister and I obeyed my mother. Even though Mother wasn't home, I started mopping the front porch every other day. I did such a good job that the neighbor told my mother that our porch "was clean enough to eat off it." That's the kind of child I was. I loved my mother dearly. Seeing her happy made me happy. I enjoyed pleasing her. Little did I know that it was a blessing in honoring your parents.

My mother set a standard for her family more by how she lived than what she said. When I became a mother I patterned my life after my mother. A godly woman, she made many sacrifices for her family and left a legacy of prayer. I am a praying woman today, because of her.

## Aunt Minnie

My mother had a sister named Minnie who would come and visit us often. Aunt Minnie had beautiful, long hair. Being a little girl, I would stand in a chair and comb her hair. One day Aunt Minnie got sick and had to come live with us. I was young and didn't know what was wrong with my aunt. My mother would prepare food for her and try to get her to eat, but she wouldn't eat it. She would just lay there like someone who was in a trance.

One night, when my mother was not at home, my great aunt Mattie came to visit with a gentleman. I remember him telling Great Aunt Mattie that she should call him because he could help Aunt Minnie. When my mother returned home that night I told her that Great Aunt Mattie had been over with a gentleman. Under the impression that Great Aunt Mattie had spoken with my mother, I informed her about the visit. Though I never understood the matter of the visit, my aunt Minnie passed away shortly thereafter. In those days, when a loved one died, the undertaker would prepare the body and visitation would take place in the home of the family. I remember when Aunt Minnie died they brought her body to our house and placed her in the living room. I felt very uncomfortable with her body there.

Later, Great Aunt Mattie came forward informing my mother of what the gentleman told her. All that time I had thought my mother knew why the gentleman wanted to see her. Now, finally after Aunt Minnie's death, Great Aunt Mattie told my mother that she brought a gentleman over to help Aunt Minnie get well. My mother became upset at the thought that her sister could still be alive had she known there was a man able to save her life. Needless to say, my mother stopped speaking to Great Aunt Mattie.

Later I overheard my great grandmother and my mother talking. I was afraid, but I still put my ear to the door to eavesdrop on their conversation. I was even more afraid when I heard them say that my aunt Minnie had a spell put on her through witchcraft. They even spoke about how it was done, who did it, and what was used to make it happen.

I was devastated. I didn't quite understand the real meaning of what happened to Aunt Minnie, but I understood enough to say, "God, please don't ever let that happen to me." But, saints of God, as time went on it did happen to me. Eventually I asked my mother to forgive Great Aunt Mattie. But deep in my heart I knew she never did.

One day, out of the blue my great aunt told me she wanted me to be the one responsible for burying her. At the time I couldn't believe she would tell me such a thing. Many years passed before Great Aunt Mattie died at 99 years old. As surprised as I had been at her request, I now consider it to have been an honor to be responsible for her burial.

**Daddy**

As a little girl I didn't understand why my daddy didn't live with us. Every time I would ask his eldest sister where he was, she would say, "Baby, I don't know where he is." When he moved from Atlanta my mother didn't know where he moved to. It seemed that nobody could (or would) tell me where he was. All I knew was that a few times, when we really needed him, he was there.

One day I overheard my mother talking about a lady my dad was involved with. For some reason the name stuck with me. Many years later I was led of God to ask my cousin the name of the lady my daddy was married to, and whether or not she was from Atlanta. When she gave me the name, it was the same name that I remembered overhearing my mother mention when I was a girl.

Years later, when God opened the door for my daddy and I to communicate, he was very sick. I received a phone call telling me that he was in the hospital. God told me to get to Detroit, go to the hospital, and pray for my dad.

Unfortunately, I told the friend I was dating at the time what God had told me to do. Sadly, I let him talk me out of going to Detroit. A short time later, my father died. I regret listening to my friend. I had to repent to God.

That's what happens when you date someone who is in darkness and you're trying to please God. If you are not strong and rooted in God their darkness will overpower you.

After attending my father's funeral, I went to his house. In the living room there was an altar. Everything on it represented the devil. I knew somebody had been practicing witchcraft. I had never seen anything like it.

## Thief in the Night

Our bed was at the window. My mother and sister slept at the head of the bed and I slept at the foot of the bed. One night, a man began breaking into our house through the window. As he was putting his foot through the window, about to step on my head, my mother woke up, screamed and scared him away. The next day my father came and fixed the window. That's when I learned that even when you're sleeping the Lord is able to protect you.

## Easter Sunday

Since Mother always did an excellent job of making us look our best, no matter what we wore, I have always been particular about the way I look. One year my dad came to our house with Easter outfits for my sister and me. When my mother took the outfits out of the bag they were both alike and so wrinkled that I did not like it. The skirt was red and the blouse was beige and the fabric was rayon. Even though my mother ironed them to perfection I still didn't feel pretty with the outfit on. I guess you could say that this experience taught me early that there were things that I definitely did NOT like. In those days, I was taught that when going to church a person should not come before God looking any kind of way. Dressing up and bringing the Lord, the King of kings, your very best was what was expected.

While I understand that the Lord is willing to let us come as we are, I still like the idea of taking pride in the way we present ourselves for worship. We are children of the Most High King, I believe we should look like it. Anyway, I chuckle inside when I think about the fact that to this day, whether dressing casual or formal, I don't buy anything made out of rayon.

## Reflections

What memories do you have from your childhood? Begin writing them here.




Were there things you didn't understand? Think about the lessons you learned as a child.

# Chapter 2 – Talent

***Lesson: Use the gifts and talents God gave you. God's favor and hard work mixed with steps of faith are an awesome combination.***

My mother was a praying woman who left a legacy of prayer. Through her, intercession was birthed in our family. As a very wise woman of God, she taught me, "never be jealous of anyone and don't try to keep up with the Jones, because you don't know what they're doing. Don't wait for anybody to give you anything, work for it."

As a child I used to watch my mother cook, clean, wash, and iron clothes. The first dish I ever cooked was cornbread and I'll never forget the first dress that I ironed. My mother was so excited that she called Ms. Laine to show the dress I had ironed. Simply watching the adults around me is how I learned to do many of the things that would develop my talents.

**Hair Stylist**

One day I stood watching my mother as she was pressing her hair with a straightening comb.

"Mother let me do that. Let me straighten your hair," I said.

She gave me the straightening comb and said, "Okay," and sat down in a chair.

Can you believe it? I started straightening my mother's hair when I was just nine years old. Sometime later, one of our neighbors gave me a pair of tin curlers.

I taught myself how to curl hair on a doll that I made from a Coca-Cola® bottle and the rope that was used to handle the ice blocks for the ice box became the hair for my doll. One day, after I felt like I had mastered curling, I said to my mother, "I can curl your hair now." She said, "Okay."

*The doll I made from the Coca-Cola® bottle looked like this.*

I used to give my mother all kinds of beautiful hair styles. Others saw the good work I did on her hair so it wasn't long before I began doing hair for many of my neighbors. In fact, at 12-years-old I had my own clientele. On a Saturday morning you would see me on my bicycle with my little paper bag that contained my tin curlers and straightening comb because I was on my way to see a client. If I shampooed a customer, the cost was $1.50. If they shampooed their own hair, the cost was $1.25. That was good money in those days.

By the age of 15, I was working in a beauty shop as a shampoo girl. One day the owner of the shop gave me a pair of Marcel curling irons and told me to learn how to use them. That day I went home and put them up and told myself that as long as I knew how to use my tin curlers I didn't need to learn how to use the Marcel curlers. Well, one day while curling a customer's hair my tin curlers broke.

Needless to say, I was forced to learn how to use the Marcel curlers and I've been using them ever since.

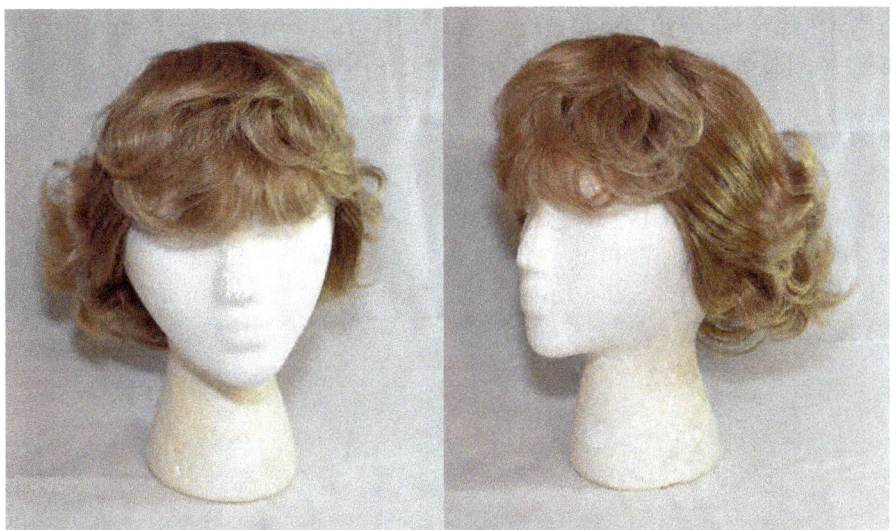

*Here is a sample of one of the styles I did for my mother.*

## Cooking

The next talent I developed was cooking. The first time I made cornbread, I put corn meal and flour in a bowl with an egg, buttermilk, some bacon drippings, and a little baking soda and my mother was amazed.

Still today God gives me recipes and instructions. For example: 1) pray over my hands to prepare the food; 2) pray over my mind to receive His visions; 3) pray over my equipment, and; 4) bless the partaker of the food. I always enjoy cooking because it is part of my ministry. I want the food to be healing to their body, and bring joy to their spirit. When my mother fell ill while living in a different state, I would cook her meals and ship them to her to make sure she not only received the correct nourishment, but also healing for her body. As a matter of fact, while writing this book I received a request for a cake and the person discussed their need of healing. So when I prepared the cake I remained in prayer over their healing. Trust me when I say, I am eagerly awaiting a praise report!

I especially enjoy cooking for Thanksgiving and Christmas. A few of my favorite recipes during that time of year are sweet potato pie, roast beef, dressing, and my famous mac and cheese. It is not unusual for me to still get out of state requests for cakes such as strawberry, cream cheese, lemon pound, and other dishes.

**Seamstress**

God also gave me the gift of sewing. I even still have the sewing machine my mother gave me for my sixteenth birthday! Yes. It works.

The Lord would show me outfits in dreams and visions. Using His visions, I would gather newspapers and cut them into the pattern I received. One year my bishop asked me to make his robe. He gave me his old robe and some material and said, "Make it." It wasn't perfect, but he wore it. Later, he gave me a pattern to go by and I got better.

In my early twenties, we were having a musical at the church and we were required to wear a black dress. Really? Because I like to be different! God showed me a dress in a dream. So, I created a pattern using newspaper and made it.

I still have that dress after all these years. It's been over fifty years since I made that dress and at age 77, I can still fit into the dress.

Before long I was sewing for different churches making usher uniforms as well as garments for other customers.

## My Own Salon

In the 1960's when I was in my twenties and still living in Atlanta, GA, I had a desire for my own salon. I was fascinated by a book entitled "The Power of Positive Thinking" by Norman Vincent Peale. After I read the book, I said to myself, "If God can do this for these people He can do it for me." Well, I found a building and as it would happen the Spirit said, "This would be a nice space for a beauty shop," and I knew the owners. I talked with them and told them what I wanted. I had no money saints. I just had faith that I could do anything after reading the book; I just knew I could. They told me I could take the space "as is" and my rent would be within my budget. But if they renovated it to be a salon then it would be more, so I decided to take it like it was.

In the meantime, the Lord sent me to this particular church. I hadn't been there long when I found out the Pastor was the owner of his own building construction company. After service on Sunday, I went to his office with $90 to ask him to renovate the space I had just purchased into a salon. He said, I've never built a salon, but I will send my crew to your shop and you can tell them what you want and they will do it for you. I went back to him the next week with my second $90 payment. He said," Ms. Holmes keep your $90." He completed the work, he contacted a bank, and set things up where I could pay the bank for the outstanding balance of $5,000 for all the work he'd done. The miracle is that God provided for me to pay back the balance so quick and fast I could not even believe it myself. I never will forget the day I was going into the bank to make the last payment and he was coming out. I said to him, "This is it, this is it; thank God this is it." I just gave God praise on how he blessed me. I kept that shop for eleven years until the Lord moved me to Michigan.

Throughout my career most of my customers' have had damaged hair. I remember praying and asking God what to do for my customers' damaged hair. I am not a scissor happy beautician so cutting it off was not all ways the answer. I asked God why do I always get customers whose hair is damaged. I always have to work so hard on their hair. He told me it was because he gave me the gift to bring dead hair back to life.

One time I was working on a customer and a new customer who had been referred walked in asking me to do her hair. As she talked to me I looked at the condition of her hair and I asked God what am I going to do to this? I didn't mind doing her hair I just didn't know what to do with it. I told her to take a seat and I would do her hair next. I finished the current client expecting her to leave, but she stayed in the shop waiting on something. I remember asking myself why is she still here? When I finished the new client and she left, the finished client that was still in the shop said," I stayed because I wanted to see what you were going to do to that." God worked a miracle.

When customers would stop coming I would cry. I knew I did an awesome job, so I would ask God what I did wrong. God said, "I sent them to bless you for a season and when their season was up I sent them to be a blessing to somebody else." Some seasons are longer than others but, I thank God that He blessed me with a successful salon.

I'm a living witness that if you use the gifts God gives you, it will not only bless your life, it will bless others too!

**Reflections**

What talents do you have?

When did you first notice them?

Have you been using them to earn a living?

# Chapter 3 – Witchcraft

**Lesson: You do not have to let other people manipulate and control your destiny!**

    I grew up in a Baptist Church until I was a teenager. At 15-years-old I was teaching Sunday school. Growing up I felt different because when I prayed for people and/or cried for them I didn't know why. It was as though I had a calling on my life for prayer. I could see a person, sense in my spirit that something was going on with them and I would begin to pray silently for them. These were my first experiences with discernment.

    I remember as a child riding the bus looking at people and I would find myself praying for them. One Sunday I was on the bus going to church. A seat next to me was vacant, then this man got on. There was something about him I didn't like. Every time I was on the bus I stared at him. If there were other vacant seats he would always choose the one next to me. I didn't like him sitting next to me.

    One day my mother came home from work very sick. She asked me to walk with her halfway to the church – I did. When she came home it was like she was never sick. The next time she went to church, I decided to go back with her because I was curious to see what was happening at the church that made her come home completely well. Wow! To my surprise the pastor of the church was the man that had been sitting next to me on the bus. If I had followed my spirit, I would have left and never went back. Later my mother stopped going to the church. I never knew what happened, but for years my Mother quit attending church altogether.

Looking back at it, I realize that it was during this time that I was learning to trust my instincts. There was a reason I didn't like him from the first time I saw him. Later, I discovered that the pastor was treating the women of the church as though they were his personal harem, taking money from them during and after church service, even showing up at their jobs. Only God knows how his wife tolerated it. That wasn't the worst of it. He also practiced witchcraft and did "work" for others.

Before I learned who he really was, even after my mother stopped going to that church, I continued to go. But, after several unexplainable crazy events happened, I began to realize that witchcraft was at work in the church. There were too many chaotic events to mention, but I will share a few of them with you:

**Ladies in The Church**

Several young ladies had nervous breakdowns and one lost her mind right there during the service. Her outbursts were so disturbing that the police were called and they handcuffed her. Another lady got pregnant by the pastor.

**Gun in The Church**

I was the godmother of an evangelist's daughter. Out of the clear, she stopped speaking to me. I couldn't think of anything I had said or done to her to make her stop speaking. I decided I was going to ask her what I did. The Lord spoke to me and said, "Don't say anything." After time passed, I decided it was time for me to say something to her, but God stopped me again. One Sunday while at morning service, many members of the congregation decided not to leave church and return for the afternoon service, but rather to remain at the church and stay for the afternoon service. This is important to me because it was the same Sunday my evangelist friend came to me and told me why she had stopped speaking. Her reason was that she was told I said something about her. She went on to say that what she was told made her so angry that she brought her gun to church to shoot me. I was shocked. When God speaks, please listen and obey. Just think, if I had disobeyed God and spoke when He instructed me not to - I might be dead.

## Fed Up

While still attending the church, in my early twenties, I became tired of being controlled by that pastor. He even had the nerve to come to my job to take my money. I had naively been giving it to him out of a desire to give to God. It was the last straw when one of the members of the church told me that he got money from me and gave it to her. After taking an overdose of pills I wrote a suicide note, which I gave to my eldest niece, who was only three years old, to give to my mother. Thank God I was rushed to the hospital, where they pumped my stomach, before I could successfully take my own life.

## Apartment Set On Fire

I met this lady minister and told her about what was going on at the church. She told me she was going to pray for me. She told me to stay in prayer because it was going to get rough, and rough it got. One day the pastor came to my house. When I let him know that he was not welcome in my house and refused to give him my money he then told me what all he was going do to my family. I confidently told him, "Whatever you do to me I rebuke it and hope it goes back to you!" The very same day he started a fire at the back door of my apartment, and stood there to watched it burn. I realized his intention was for me not to leave the apartment alive. But God gave me supernatural strength. I got pass him, ran next door, and asked my neighbor if I could use her phone (there were no cell phones in those days). I called his wife and told her to come and get her husband because he was at my house going crazy.

I never went back to that church. At that time I hated him with a passion. However, some years later God told me, "You must forgive him so I can continue to bless you." Needless to say, I forgave the man. I'm not losing out on God's blessing in my life for nobody!

**Beware!**

Witchcraft is like a ball; when you've sent it out, it bounces back to the sender, and it's more powerful when it returns. Although witchcraft is powerful, it is not as powerful as God's power. I thank God that He took care of me. He kept my mind. I am alive to tell you that God is all powerful. Just like the story of Job in the Bible. God asked satan if he had considered his servant Job; satan reminded God that He had a hedge around him. God removed the hedge and told satan not to touch his soul. When Job went through he came out with the victory. If you stay connected to the vine, which is Jesus Christ, nothing will be able to separate you from Him. Pray, read His word daily, and be filled with the Holy Spirit.

Some people say that witchcraft is not real and it can't do anything. Oh, yes it can. I am a living witness. But, I'm also a witness that God will keep you in the midst of it. My mind was supposed to been gone many years ago, but God has kept my mind, and He has also kept my body. I can't even tell you how hard I used to work while my head hurt. I went to the doctor and he couldn't find out what was wrong, so I just stopped going. I made God my doctor and He has taken care of me all these 77 years. I thank God that He didn't let this servant die from witchcraft.

Those of you who are into witchcraft, I pray that you repent because you will never receive all of the blessings that God has for you. For those of you that are in a church and it's not prosperous and you aren't growing and becoming prosperous you need to go before God for a new church home.

**Reflections**
Have you ever experienced unexplainable hindrances?




Have others ever taken unfair advantage of your lack of knowledge about God? If so, how have you grown?

Have you ever felt that others were bypassing your right to make choices through manipulation or other works of the flesh? See Galatians 5.

# Chapter 4 – The Challenges of Adulthood

**Lesson: God is ALWAYS worthy of praise and worship; even when other people hurt you.**

It was the late '60's and I was in my late twenties. I was completely sold out to God. It was me and Jesus; so much so that He was working miracles through me. Whatever we do, we need to keep that close relationship with the Lord. But, if we're not careful satan will sneak in.

One day I was at home, minding my own business, and my doorbell rang. When I looked out of the door, it was one of the brothers from my church. When I opened the door he had brought one of his friends to meet me. What a package! He was my type. Though divorced, his friend was a college graduate, very handsome, smart, well dressed, well trained, and quiet. But he was not the Lord's type. Even though I knew he did not have a relationship with God, we began dating. Big mistake.

I had been serving God. He had not. Anyway, there I was, light in a relationship with darkness. Before long, I let him move in with me; another big mistake. I started partying, going to night clubs and wearing mini-dresses. One day I went before God to receive instructions from Him and I couldn't hear anything. God had stopped talking to me. Can you imagine how I felt? I had to learn the hard way.

Even though we got engaged, we never did get married. He ended up moving back to his hometown to go into business. Even though we are still friends, to this day he is not married and lives with his mother, taking excellent care of her. In fact, his mother and I have a relationship to this day. Anyway angels, please do not jeopardize your relationship with God. No man is worth it!

In 1975, I received prophecy that I was going to get out of debt so I started working hard to get out of debt. But at the end of 1975, but I was still in debt.

In February 1976, I dreamt I was in church; this lady came to me and began to prophesy to me. She said, "be very careful, I see you getting pregnant." I said to her, "Who me?" She said," Yes, you." She kept saying to me, "the baby is going to be a blessing to you, the baby is going to be a blessing to you." The next morning, I called my girlfriend and

*Here I am with friends when I was pregnant with Jonique.*

told her the dream. She said, "You better watch that dream." I said, "Girl, I am not going to get pregnant."

At that time, I was modeling through Model's Touch which was located on Campbellton Road in Atlanta. I went out of town on a modeling assignment, though I was not feeling well. April came and I was pregnant. I was very upset because of my age and because I was not married. I became very worried about what people were going to think about me. But I realized that people were already talking about me and people were going to talk whether it's good or bad. I decided I was going to have my baby.

*Look at my baby! Isn't she adorable?*

What a blessing my daughter is to me. She's beautiful, smart, and talented. She is a school teacher and she loves the heavenly Father. As a matter of fact, when I got pregnant, the Lord spoke to me, "I am going to show you how to get out of debt, get paper and pen." By the time my baby was born I was out of debt. December 31, 1976, God blessed us tremendously where I owed no man and was able to provide for my daughter as a single parent. I had a good savings account and lived an affluent life style. I was living in downtown Atlanta in Colony Square on 15th street.

January 4, 1979, God blessed me to be baptized and filled with the Holy Spirit. Since then my life began to take a different direction. When my daughter was a year old I had been in my salon in Atlanta for 11 years and God told me to sell it and go to Michigan. I told God I didn't want to live in Michigan; to visit yes but to live no, so I didn't move to Michigan. I told God things were going to work out.

My daughter's father passed on February 19, 1979, right after she turned two years old. The next year I gave her a birthday party. After the Lord spoke in a clear voice and said," I want you to take your baby, with the $1,500 you have saved, go to the city of Detroit and I want you to trust me." I screamed out loud," Yes Lord, I'll go." I ran to the telephone and called Minister Sapp and told her what the Lord had spoken to me. Minister Sapp said, "Yes I know, I was praying that you would call me because I have some scriptures that I want to give you to cherish always." It was Deuteronomy 28 and Proverbs 3. I moved to Michigan on January 13, 1980.

In the 80's I used to go home on my break between customers to watch soap operas. The Lord spoke to me and asked," why are you coming home to watch soap operas, you should be coming home to pray." As a result, I started asking my customers and co-workers if they had any prayer requests. I would bring them home and pray over them. God answered many prayers and worked many miracles.

## Life in Michigan

Having established myself in Michigan, I found a church that I loved attending. Not only did it have a beautiful building with a large congregation, the worship services were filled with lively worship music and the Word of God was preached with great power. I was growing in my relationship with God and prospering in my business.

One day in prayer, God told me to start visiting other churches. "God, it's too many churches here. Where will I start?" I asked. The following Sunday I called a friend in Atlanta. As I talked with her she said, "I don't know why I'm telling you this, but there is a church I want you to visit." I told her that God had told me to start visiting other churches and He was giving me a place to start. Then she gave me the name and address of the church.

Monday, I asked my neighbor to help me find the address. When I went to the church I sat in the car looking at the church. I couldn't believe my eyes.

"God, are you telling me to leave my big pretty church, to come to this dinky-dink looking church?"

"Didn't I send you to Michigan and tell you to trust me?" He asked.

"Yes," I responded.

"Then trust me now," He said.

Wednesday morning, God gave me a vision and showed me the inside of the church. I saw the leader and his wife. I even saw that she was more anointed than he was. So Sunday came and my daughter and I went to the new church. When I got to there, everything was just as God had shown me. During the service God told me to buy the church a new drum set.

"God, I don't have the money," I said, as if He didn't know what I had.

"I'm going to bless you with it," He said. "Now go tell the pastor that I said you are to buy a new set of drums."

I told the pastor what God told me. He was so excited. "Praise the Lord!" he shouted. Then the pastor told me about how a white minister had told the church to begin praising God because He was going to send someone to buy a new set of drums for the church. I bought the drums with no idea about the how God intended to bless me there.

**Marriage - The Unexpected Blessing**

Later God showed me that He was going to fill up the little church. But, every time it was about to get full I would look up and the people were gone. I didn't understand.

Around that time, God started showing me a man in my dreams. I saw his skin color and his unusual side burns. He also told me that it was time to leave the big beautiful church I loved. I didn't want to leave.

One day my sister called me and told me how her daughter had given birth to a baby boy. But that wasn't her real reason for calling.

"I really called you because God told me to call you. He has a blessing for you, but it is not in the church you are in."

I knew that word was from God, because I had not been talking to my sister.

The following Sunday my daughter and I went to the new church. When the pastor opened the doors of the church I knew I had to join. As my daughter and I stood at the altar with the other people, who do you think came and stood beside us? I was amazed to see the man God had shown me in my dreams. It had to be him, there was no mistaking those unusual side burns. I said to myself, "God, that's him! That's him!" Even though I knew he would be my husband, I made no effort to meet him. Later in November, one of the ministers in the church introduced me to Bro. Singleterry and we began dating. In December he proposed. January 25th we had a large wedding. The church was filled and running over all the way to the balcony, just as God had shown me.

**Let God Check Everything Out**

In my earlier years I had said that I would never marry a man without "checking him out." But God knows how to change your mind.

One day while in prayer the Lord told me not to have sex until I was married. I asked, "Lord, what if he wants to check me out?" "Leave it to me," the Lord replied.

Two days later, my husband to be said, "Let's not have sex until we are married."

Because He made us, God really does know everything about you. I am a living witness that He knows just what you like and how you like it. Amen. Amen, and Amen.

## Marriage Troubles

As much as I appreciated all the good things about my husband, I never cried as much I did after I got married. Everything went wrong. I lost my credit, I lost my big savings account. I lost other money, and I could hardly buy groceries. Every week I would call my loved one and tell her that something just wasn't right.

One day I was standing at the sink and it felt like a thousand ants were crawling up and down my feet and legs. I began to run and jump. I looked down and I didn't see anything. I knew something was wrong. As time passed I began to really suffer with my feet. I could hardly walk and I had to work in house shoes.

One night, I asked God what was wrong with my feet. God showed me my feet and it scared me to death. Nobody knew how I suffered. I would go to bed sick and wake up sick with horrible headaches. I don't know how I worked, drove my car, and took care of my husband and daughter; except to say that God helped me. I suffered so much that I was sick all the time. But, I kept up a front so nobody would know how I really felt. I worked long and hard hours because I didn't have the support that I needed from my husband.

One day, my loved one called me and said that she went to a prophetess for herself. The Lord showed me to the prophetess and told her everything. She knew the prophetess was right because of what I'd been telling her every week. She told her what to tell me to do. I went before God and I said," I am not going to do what my loved one told me to do. Instead I am leaving this in your hand to take care of my husband, my daughter, and me." And my God did. Saints, don't fight your battles, give them to God. He can handle it in Jesus' name. When He has given you His Spirit, you aren't afraid of the devil. Get in your secret place and pray. If you don't know what to say, pray the Lord's Prayer.

There were times I asked God, "Why did You tell me to marry him? What was I to learn from this marriage?" One thing I did know, marriage took a lot of patience, as time went on I learned to walk in it. I used to ask God how long do I have to suffer. I thought about how Job suffered, but he didn't give up. He kept praising and worshipping his God. Saints, that's what I do because at times I still go through things, but I know I have the victory.

**Kicked Out of the Church**

We visited a church several times attempting to determine if it should be our new home. We enjoyed the prayer services and the way the Word of God was brought forth. The interesting thing about this church was the attire of some of the congregation. Being a family of the Most High God, a family of the King, we always made it a point to dress and carry ourselves, especially on Sunday, in our best attire. It was a family decision for us to coordinate our outfits in color and style. Eventually we joined the church. We also worked in the church; I was a tape counselor and my husband was an extremely dedicated and creative catechism teacher. He would spend endless hours developing visual aids and study material to not only educate but to also create curiosity and keep attendees engaged. How God used him was simply amazing. Even the Bishop told him he was called into the ministry. My family and I had a relationship with the Bishop, even to the point where he would call and ask me, "What has the Lord been saying to you lately?"

December 31, 1989, two years after joining the church, during Sunday morning service, we were worshipping and praising God. But, when the Bishop entered the pulpit I could tell something was on his mind. I had called him the week before and he never returned my call. I knew that was strange. When praise and worship was over we were still standing; church was full of about 1,000 people. When he called my name I thought that he was going to prophesy to me. He said, "You and your family find yourself another church." We were all standing; my husband and I gripped hands; we couldn't move. "And don't stand there like you don't know what I'm talking about," he continued. I thought, "Lord, I don't know what he's talking about." We stayed until the service was over and nobody said anything to us. When we got in the car we were speechless. We never did confront him; we were too hurt. As the days went by we replayed the incident and searched our minds as to why he would do such a thing. After not coming up with the answer, those hurt feelings turned into hate.

A member told me she spoke to the Bishop and told him he was wrong and he owed us an apology. According to her, the Bishop said, "Jesus didn't apologize." When she told me what he said, my response was "who told him he was Jesus?"

My daughter was 13 years old when this happened, and until this day she doesn't go to church.

**God's Blessing in Spite of...**

Friends had heard and those I told about the incident starting recommending churches for us to visit. The last church on the list was Agape. When we walked in, we felt the love of God. So in 1990 we joined Agape. In 1991, Sunday morning service was awesome. While worshiping, God carried me and I had an open vision. In this vision I was suspended overlooking the congregation of my previous church – the one where my family was asked to leave. "Lord, are you telling me to go back to that church?" I asked. "No," He replied, "but I want you to forgive the Bishop. Because of your unforgiving spirit I can't bless you. There are blessings I want to give you." At that moment I fell to my knees. When I got up I knew in my heart I had forgiven him.

The blessings God was referring to, was Him establishing a bond between me and my daughter. I called myself retiring from doing hair to start a catering business. Well, that didn't last long. It was too much hard work because my staff was unreliable, so I said, "Lord, what's next?"

Finally, I returned to doing hair. A customer called me and asked what product she could buy to use on her hair. A couple of weeks later she called me at home this time asking what kind of straightening comb to buy. I said, "Angel when I get through making my delivery come over and I will do your hair." It was as though God took my words into the atmosphere because the phone started ringing and customers told me they hadn't gotten their hair fixed in a long time. So when I finished my deliveries I would tell them to come over and I would do their hair. When the customers were leaving they said we will see you in two weeks, and I said, "let me pray about it." I went before God and I said, "God you did say you were going to establish a bond between me and my daughter could this be it? I can do hair in my home and the answer was, "yes."

God gave me instructions on what to do. My daughter was very happy. I was there when she left home in the morning to go to school and there when she came home. What a blessing that was to work in the home and be available for my daughter. I even had time to do volunteer work at her school and go to P.T.A. meetings.

God used me to minister to my customers. Because I had them to bring their bible so we could have personal prayer time, ladies gave their lives to Christ. I taught ladies how to cook, and when they saw how clean and neat my house was, they told me they were now keeping their house clean and neat. I thank God that I was able to be a blessing.

I didn't want to return back to the shop. I had a lot of prayer time for myself and I didn't want it to end. When my time was up, my daughter released me to go back to the shop. God did great bonding with my daughter and me.

## Reflections

What challenges have you had to face?

How did you handle them?

*Chapter 4 – The Challenges of Adulthood*

Are you facing challenges now? If so, write them down here. Then begin praising and worshipping God while believing He will answer you.

# Chapter 5 – Becoming a Worshipper

***Lesson: When you don't have a clue how things will work out, praise, worship, and serve God anyway.***

Monday, June 13, 1994, before daybreak God spoke to me saying, "Gwen, I know everything about you; I know your needs. I don't want you to ask me for anything. All I want you to do is <u>praise</u> me, <u>worship</u> me, and <u>give Me thanks</u>." Saints that's the key to becoming a worshipper.

Tuesday, June 14, 1994, I came home from work; I began to go through my house worshipping, praising, and giving God the praise. God gave me instructions to go to a particular boutique and tell a particular woman to give me 30 days (same as cash) credit. God told me He was going to dress me to look like a queen.

Wednesday, June 15, 1994, I went to that boutique and the person God instructed me to speak with stated she was glad to see me and she had been praying for customers. I then told her what God said and she followed His instructions. She went on to offer me 45 days credit or however long I wanted and that I had no limit on the credit. I paid for the items, even though she never told me the terms of the agreement or how to pay. Now when I need something I no longer ask God, I automatically begin to thank Him that my need has been met.

**Debt-Free Education**

God has an interesting way of getting blessings to us. My husband was never the type of man to provide financial support which meant I had the burden of paying the bills. It was not uncommon for us to have more bills than money which ultimately led to my bank account being closed due to incurring significant insufficient funds charges. After several months God told me to go back to the bank and open a new account. I told God I couldn't go back because I still owed money. God stated that He wiped my record clean and I did not owe any money. I returned to the bank and opened an account. And just as God told me, there was no record of my negative financial transactions.

When making a transaction one day, the supervisor checked my account for available funds and noticed I kept making deposits through the ATM. The bank supervisor advised that since I tend to withdraw the money to pay bills almost immediately after the deposit, the best thing to do is to stop using the ATM to deposit the money because it took too many days to post to my account. Instead, put the money in their night deposit box and it would post to my account immediately. Her recommendation made a huge difference with me not incurring insufficient funds charges. To show her my appreciation I started baking cakes and delivering them to her at the bank. She began sharing my cakes with the tellers and told me how much they liked the cakes. I then began baking cakes for the tellers for free.

During the time my daughter was in high school God would speak to me concerning her education. One day while riding down Northwestern Highway going home from work, the Lord spoke to me and said He wanted my daughter to have a debt-free college education. I was shocked. I asked Him, "How do I do that when I am barely making ends meet now?" Right before my daughter graduated from high school God began to show me how to put money aside for her college education. By the time she got accepted into college we had saved enough to pay for her 1st year of tuition. But God didn't stop there, He sent people to prosper my way such as my mother who paid 1 year of tuition and continued to use her all through my daughter's college years.

On one occasion God told me to write a check for $1,000 for my daughter's tuition. I didn't have the money. God told me to trust Him, "Write the check, and mail it. By the time the check makes it to your bank the money will be there." To my amazement the money was there, just like He said.

In the midst of my daughter's last year of college, I needed money for tuition, rent and other bills totaling $4,000.00 dollars. I wrote a check for it all and had no money to cover them; I had faith.

As a result, the bank supervisor called me at work and said," Gwen, you had checks totaling $4,000 come in and there is no money in your account." I said, "I know." She said," I tell you what I do know, you are a hard worker so I'm going to put my job on the line for you. I'm going to pay every one of these checks." I said to her," I promise I will pay back every dime in two weeks." God gave me $4,000 to cover those checks and all she wanted in return was the recipe to my pound cake.

I was so excited about how God blessed my daughter with a debt-free education, I shared my testimony with anyone that would listen. One day my customer and I were going shopping and on the way I mentioned to her how God gave my daughter a debt-free education. She said, "I needed to hear that because I have a son ready for college but my husband said he could not go because we cannot afford the tuition." A few months later she telephoned me to let me know that she was stepping out on faith to send their son to college. Her son went to undergraduate college debt-free. He then went on to graduate from Tuskegee University Veterinary Medical School on May 7, 2015.

***Man and Mirror***

In the late 90's, I worked at a beautiful salon. I had my own private suite and over the shampoo bowl was a beautiful and heavy mirror.

I had a customer who was a minister. She called and cancelled her appointment because she said the Lord was calling her and the church into a 3-day fast and shut-in. However, before the fast and shut-in started a member from her church came in for an appointment. I asked how they were fasting. She told me it was 3 days of water and juice from Thursday 6:00PM until Sunday 6:00AM and they would end the fast by drinking milk and honey. After hearing how they did the fast, God told me to join their fast on Thursday and instead of being shut-in because I needed to keep working He told me to pray.

The next day while still on the fast was Friday. I was shampooing my customer when the Lord spoke to me and said, "Call in the assistant and tell him how you want him to blow dry her hair." I thought, "there's no need to tell him how to dry her hair because she does not have a chemical relaxer, so it doesn't matter what direction he dried her hair." I kept working and the Lord spoke to me again very firm saying, "Call him in here." When He spoke firmly, I called the assistant in and he stood on the opposite side of the shampoo bowl where the mirror hung. Before I could say anything to him, I happened to look up and see the mirror falling. I caught one side and he caught the other. We both stood there in shock not saying a word. After that, my customer opened her eyes and the assistant finally took the mirror and sat it outside my suite. When God tells you to do something, no matter what it is just do it, because there is a reason He's saying to do it. I believe God told me to call in the assistant because He knew the mirror was going to fall which could have killed my customer.

When I left the salon that evening, I stopped to pick a meal up for my family. As I was making their plates, staring at the chicken so hard because it smelled and looked so good, the Lord asked me, "Is that chicken worth giving up your fast?" I said, "No." After that three day fast many blessings materialized.

## The Blessing of Answered Prayers

God began to speak to me to have prayer in my home. So, I stopped working on Saturday. Saints you know that was a big step of faith. A hair stylist's busiest day is Saturday. But I know my God is worthy, so I began having prayer meeting with the ladies. I even made refreshments. For quite a while God blessed the ladies through the meeting; until my church began to prepare for catechism graduation on the same day. Though I didn't return to the prayer meeting after that, I continue to pray with and for others as the Lord directs me.

Years ago when vegetables used to be packed in plastic bags I had a taste for turnip greens. When I went to the store they did not look good at all. But, since I wanted them so bad I took a chance. When I got to the cash register the cashier picked up the greens and flipped them over. Frowning at me she said, "Are you going to buy these?" I didn't know what to say so I just stood there.

After I got home and got my daughter settled I opened the bag of greens. I was shocked. The greens on the outside looked horrible, but the greens on the inside were the most beautiful greens I'd ever seen. The Lord began to speak to me. "See Gwen, just like with these greens, you cannot judge a person by the outside. You need the gift of discernment to see past the natural man. If you had gone by what you saw you would not have had any greens."

I recall one instance where my co-worker told me her aunt had gone to the doctor and was diagnosed with cancer. Four days later God instructed me to go and pray for my co-worker's aunt. I didn't want to go, because I believed her nieces would talk bad about me. But, it's always best to obey God. I went to her aunt's house and told her that God had sent me there to pray for her. She gave her consent. Weeks later when she went for a checkup, there was no cancer! God had healed her! Praise God!!!

In my eldest nephew's early life, he was diagnosed with an incurable disease and was hospitalized. God gave me instructions, "Go to Atlanta and do not tell anybody anything. When you leave the airport, take a taxi and go to the hospital. Pray for him, but do not sit all day with him. Leave before anyone else gets there." When visitors started coming he told them that I had been there and prayed for him. They thought he was out of his mind. Later that evening I showed up at my mother's house and they were shocked.

In this walk with God, we cannot always tell everything God tells us. There comes a time we need to ask Him to help us bridle our tongue – Psalm 39:1.

## Reflections

As you look back over your life, what experiences have caused you to stop and worship God?

Can you remember where His timing and wisdom saved you from calamity?

# Chapter 6 – Life Moves You Around

*Lesson: No matter where life takes you, God is there.*

**Taking Care of My Mother**

In June of 2000, my daughter graduated from college, and God told me to plan her graduation party immediately. July of that same year, my niece called and said that my mother needed help. I knew if my mother needed help it was serious so I started making plans to move to Atlanta to take care of my mother. I made an appointment with a storage company that also packed and moved items. The appointment date was August 21st. But before I could attend the appointment I received a call from my niece telling me my mother was to have brain surgery. The next morning the Lord spoke to me and said, "This is your last working day; go see about your mother." I called the storage company and told them I had an emergency and needed to move immediately. The gentleman told me he could not help me because of the short notice but he would call his friend that had a storage company. The friend he called contacted me and stated he would be at my home on Friday morning to help me move and place my items at his storage company.

We packed all night. Some items I put in storage and other items I packed to move to Atlanta such as my appointment book. I went to Atlanta trusting my God.

I made it to my mother's house, God proceeded to tell me there was a special place in the basement and He wanted me to meet Him there. And every time we met He spoke some awesome things with me.

## Acknowledging Sin is Key

One thing God spoke to me during that time was to apologize to someone. I told Him, "God, I can't do that!" A couple of weeks later, He told me again, "Go and apologize." When He spoke to me about it the second time, I knew I needed to go and apologize. Just like in the Bible when God confronted King David, through His prophet Nathan, about his sinful behavior with another man's wife, I had to acknowledge my sin.

In my earlier adulthood, I had an affair with a married man. Imagine my shock when, years later, God told me to call his wife and apologize for interfering in her marriage. It was an even bigger surprise when she forgave me. Angels, God can give you the power and strength to face the sins of your past, if you let Him. And when you obey Him, you open the door for Him to bring peace where you thought there could never be any.

## No Alcohol for Christmas

I remember once during the time I was taking care of my mother, I cooked Thanksgiving dinner and I made a dessert that required rum. I had some left over so I called my customer for her rum cake recipe. I decided that I would make a rum cake for Christmas.

In the meantime, I bought the tape by Juanita Bynum *Behind the Veil*. After I put Mother to bed, I played the tape. I began to worship and praise God so much so that I was on the floor. God began to talk to me.

"Have you ever made a rum cake for your birthday?" He asked.

"No, Lord," I responded.

"Then why do you want to make one on My birthday?"

I screamed and cried, "I'm sorry Lord!"

Though I still sometimes use alcohol when cooking my food, I never do for Christmas. In fact, once God asked me, "Why do you give gifts to everyone but Me at Christmas?" Whenever I've had the opportunity I've recommended that people prepare a special envelope to give a monetary gift for God, so He can receive a gift at Christmas.

## Sowing Seeds and Answered Prayers for My Mother

One morning as I was getting ready for church, I heard a minister on the television challenging listeners to believe God by sowing a seed for the blessing they wanted to receive. I decided to sow a seed for my mother to walk. Later that week, she called the nurse to help her to go the bathroom. When the nurse came she asked her to hold her hand because she believed she could walk. Sure enough, she walked to the bathroom. Later that same day my mother went to therapy and she walked even more. Praise God! When my mother came home from the hospital, though she needed assistance, she was walking.

During the time after I returned to Atlanta to care for my mother, my eldest niece would come to visit. She would get on the bed with Mother and sing to her. One day as my mother talked with me about how much she enjoyed my niece's singing, she mentioned that she would like me to sing too. "I can't sing," I responded, "but I can pray." Every night I would pray with my mother or pray over her. What a joy it was to see healing take place!

*Mother and I*

My mother would ring a bell at night when she needed to get up. I continued to pray with her, especially for strength. Before I knew it she was getting up and walking **on her own**.

## God Works Everything Out

One night I had a dream that I was booking appointments one after another. I asked the Lord, "What does this mean." A week later on Monday, I received a phone call from one of my customers from Michigan. She said," Gwen, there is no one here to do our hair like you do." Wednesday, I had to take the car to the dealer; they didn't have the part I needed. My husband decided to talk to a dealer in Michigan and they said to bring the car up there. Having heard that, I called my customer back and told her that I will be in Michigan for two days. I called the owner of the shop in Michigan and asked if my booth was still available. He said, "Yes". I told him I would like to work Friday and Saturday and he said okay and he would not charge me booth rent. Now having a place to work in Michigan, I began to call other customers letting them know I could work on Friday and Saturday. Before I knew it I was booking customers almost every Friday and Saturday. Working that much took time away from helping my mother, but we needed the income. I prayed on how to get help and the Lord instructed me to call my daughter living in Chicago and I asked her to rush her plans to come to Atlanta and help care for my mother. By my daughter helping with my mother, it allowed me to fly once a month to Michigan, which soon became every two weeks, then every week.

One of my customers said," Miss Gwen, let's send out a letter asking your customers to give $10 - $15 towards your plane ticket." The Lord spoke to me and said," No. I will tell those ladies what to pay you for their hair." And Saints of God that's what He did. My customers started paying $50 to $300 to do their hair. God blessed me to travel from Georgia to Michigan to do hair for 5 years and 6 months, all while caring for my husband and mother who were sick at the same time. I worked hard and long hours to provide for my family and pay for their hospital bills. I was starting at 4:00 A.M. and sometimes earlier. God gave me supernatural strength in my body. I could not have done all of this if it were not for God; He is AWESOME!

I remember one time when God blessed me with money. I was so excited. I put my clothes on getting ready to walk out the door. God said, "You didn't ask Me what to do with the money." I sat down and went to sleep. When I woke up He instructed me exactly what to do. I thank God for stopping me because I would have never thought to use the money that way. Angels, don't forget to consult God about EVERYTHING!

**Consult God about EVERYTHING!**

After battling cancer for a year, my husband transitioned in 2003 and my mother transitioned in 2005 from a bowel eruption. I received notification regarding my husband's insurance policy, which I received and spent on providing for my relatives. I dealt with lawyers dealing with my mother's money and received no money at all. As I wept asking God, "How is it that being a giver and taking care of my family that I am destitute?"

He answered, "You never asked me what you should do with the money. You acted on your own."

Saints, this is what happens when you fail to consult God. This was a lesson well learned. Now I wait for God to tell me what to do. After repenting for wasting the money, when getting off the elevator God spoke to me and said He would give me everything I wanted, but I would have to be patient. I said, "God you know I don't' have patience." Although they both were gone I still worked as a beautician traveling from Georgia to Michigan.

May 5, 2007, after realizing that most of my clients were in Michigan, I moved there with no money, no credit and no car because I was still trying to recoup from the bad financial decisions I made without consulting God. But the things I did have were faith and patience. Remember I told you God taught me that when I am in need of something I should not ask Him for what I am in need of, but rather praise him for providing me with what I need. Well I did exactly that. I didn't ask God for what I needed, instead I praised, worshipped and gave thanks to Him.

While being patient and having faith, I was on the telephone with one customer, while working on another customer. The customer that was in my chair overheard my telephone conversation. She said, "Miss Gwen does your other customer need a car?" I said, "Yes and so do I."

She responded, "I have someone who will help you." Later that day she contacted a car salesman and told me to give him a call. I talked with him, and I told him I didn't have any credit, I just wanted a car to drive and oddly enough I never told him what type of car I wanted. He said he would work with me and, "you keep praying." I was very patient. At the end of two weeks, God blessed me with a 2004 Jaguar, clean with low mileage. It is now paid for and I give God the glory.

**Throwing in the Towel**

I thank God for His love for me because it stopped me from taking matters into my hands regarding so many different areas of my life. It was a Tuesday morning, February 13, 2013, when God woke me up and he told me get up and go in the living room to lay on the floor and pray. As I began to pray God said, "Remember Abraham and Sarah and I told them they were going to have a son. Sarah became impatient and she decided to take matters into her own hands so she gave her handmaid to her husband. And from that night a son was born. Do you remember how Sarah regretted what she had done? It made a mess of the lives for everyone involved. If you take matters into your hands, you will regret it." Still to this day, Sarah's decision is still causing trouble for many nations. I thank God for His love for me and how He takes time to minister to me.

Patience is an act of confidence that all is unfolding as it should even when the process takes longer than we had hoped or expected. Patience is not lazy or indifferent. You don't have to push or force a result in order to feel that you are making progress. Just as a farmer cannot hurry or worry a harvest into existence, we cannot rush results that must be unfolded in their own time.

## Chapter 6 – Life Moves You Around

True patience is silent energy; one that restores and strengthens. I deny power to any feeling or doubt or impatience. And while I wait, I pray. I stay focused on the present moment expecting the greater good to come. I remind myself of how long Joseph had to wait, and in his waiting, he continued to serve the Lord, and he did not lose faith.

I praise God for Jeremiah 29:11:

*For I know the thoughts that I think toward you, says the Lord, thoughts of peace and not of evil, to give you a future and a hope.*

I know God has a plan for us. What is the attitude of your heart toward your problem? God has permitted the problem to exist for a purpose so we can rest assured that He is working something out in our lives. God tests our faith with the purpose of growing patience. And having gone through the process I have learned that patience will help you to grow and mature. It is for this reason God wants to do work in our lives so we can become strong Christians in this generation.

I thank God that He knows all of my shortcomings. He knows the things that hinder us from His plan that He has for us. God knew I needed patience to reach my destiny. This has been an awesome journey. I thank God for working with me along the way. There were times I didn't think I was going to make it. He didn't let me give up. I praise God and appreciate the ending that led to my new beginnings. I give thanks that the presence of God is in every experience. I thank God for the knowledge and wisdom that I have learned while walking this journey of patience. I have set my focus in the Word of God and His promises. Now I have discovered his abundance of joy, peace, and prosperity in every area of my life. With patience come peace, joy, happiness, love, and stability as we continue to walk this journey. God will turn every problem around and take you to a higher level of faith.

I am experiencing the blessing of walking in patience. It is a mind blower. This journey of patience has been very rewarding, and 2015 gave me a profound sense of patience.

**Habakkuk 2:3**-*For the vision is yet for an appointed time, but at the end it shall speak, and not lie: though it tarry, wait for it; because it will surely come, it will not tarry. The revelation awaits an appointed time. It speaks of the end and will not prove false. Though it lingers, wait for it. It will certainly come and will not delay.*

God has a storehouse of blessings that He has reserved for you and me. Our time to receive these blessings may not be the same as our Lord's. God has a specific time that He requires to accomplish His purpose in the life of the believer. Sometimes that will mean going through seasons that seem excruciatingly cruel and painful, yet it is needful.

When we read that Joseph remained a slave in Egypt and then was placed in prison after being wrongfully accused, it would be easy to second guess God. Oh how cruel and uncaring, we might think. Joseph thought he was going to be delivered from prison when he interrupted a dream from a court official. Instead he was forgotten for another two years. Why? An early release would have disrupted God's perfect plan. God takes time to develop character before anything else. God could not afford to have a prideful 30-year-old managing the resources of an entire region of the world. We can sometimes delay this time, if we refuse his correction.

Although, it is sometimes difficult to understand God's love during the waiting period, try to remember that the Lord is just and gracious in His dealing with his children. When He does decide to move on our behalf, we will appreciate the delay and will often understand the reason it was needed. "For the Lord is a God of justice, and blessed are the ones who wait on him." (Isaiah 30:18)

## Reflections

Having read my testimonies of God's goodness, what memories of God's faithfulness have you remembered? Use the following pages and take a moment to write them down and don't forget to share them with others.

In what ways has God shown His faithfulness to you?

# Chapter 7 – Scripture to Stand On

**Lesson: God's Word will work to change your life better than anything else in the world.**

While it is true that the entire Bible is filled with instructions worthy of our attention, the ones I picked to share here are some my favorites. Meditate on them. They will bring you comfort, wisdom, and instructions that will help you to persevere as you wait patiently upon God.

**Romans 15:5** - Now may the God of patience and comfort grant you to be like-minded toward one another, according to Jesus Christ.

**Psalms 40:1-3** - I waited patiently for the Lord; and he inclined to me, and heard my cry. He also brought me up out of a horrible pit, out of the miry clay, and set my feet upon a rock, and established my steps. He has put a new song in my mouth.

**Hebrews 6:12** - That you do not become sluggish, but imitate those who through faith and patience inherit the promises.

**Hebrews 10:36-37** - For you have need of endurance, so that after you have done the will of God, you may receive the promise: For yet a little while and he who is coming will come and will not tarry.

**James 1:3-4** - Knowing that the testing of your faith produces patience. But let patience have its perfect work, that you may be perfect and complete, lacking nothing.

**Roman 8:28** - And we know that all things work together for good to those who love God, to those who are the called according to his purpose.

**James 5:10-11** - My brethren, take the prophets, who spoke in the name of the Lord as an example of suffering and patience. Indeed we count them blessed who endure. You have heard of the perseverance of Job and seen the end intended by the Lord that the Lord is very compassionate and merciful.

**James 5:8** - You also be patient. Establish your hearts, for the coming of the Lord is at hand.

**Psalms 37:7-9** - Rest in the Lord and wait patiently for him; do not fret because of him who prospers in his way. Because of the man who brings wicked schemes to pass. Cease from anger, and forsake wrath; do not fret it only causes harm. For evildoers shall be cut off; but those who wait on the Lord they shall inherit the earth.

**Colossians 1:9b-11** - ...desire that ye might be filled with the knowledge of his will in all wisdom and spiritual understanding; That ye might walk worthy of the Lord unto all pleasing, being fruitful in every good work, and increasing in the knowledge of God; Strengthened with all might, according to his glorious power, unto all patience and longsuffering with joyfulness;

**1 Corinthians 10:13** - No temptation has overtaken you except such as is common to man; but God is faithful, who will not allow you to be tempted beyond what you are able, but with the temptation will also make the way of escape, that you may be able to bear it.

**Luke 8:15** - But the ones that fell on the good ground are those who having heard the word with a noble and good heart, keep it and bear fruit with patience.

**Jeremiah 29:11** - For I know the thoughts that I think toward you, says the Lord, thoughts of peace and not of evil, to give you a future and a hope.

**Isaiah 30:18** - Therefore the Lord will wait that he may be gracious to you and therefore he will be exalted that he may have mercy on you. For the Lord is a God of justice; blessed are all those who wait for him.

**Revelation 3:10** - Because you have kept my command to persevere, I also will keep you from the hour of trial which shall come upon the whole world, to test those who dwell on the earth.

# Photo Album

*Here's a picture from my modeling days.*

*My mother, daughter Jonique, and I*

*My husband and I on a cruise.*

*A dear church mother gave me this hat!*
*God bless you Mother Lillie!*

# Encouraging Words

## to

## Live By

*Prayer is VERY important! Never forget to ask God what is His Will.*

**ALWAYS make time to study God's Word!**

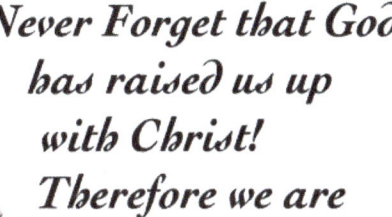

**Never Forget that God has raised us up with Christ! Therefore we are SEATED in heavenly places in Christ Jesus!**

**Remember... God's goodness and love makes you blessed and highly favored!**

*Never Forget that you are NOT alone! There are others in the Body of Christ who are committed to helping you fulfill God's purpose in you!*

My book coach, Christina Dixon, and I

# About the Author

Gwendolyn Singleterry is a woman whose faith in God has seen her through over 70 years of life. As a young girl her love for her mother, coupled with ingenuity and an excellent work ethic gained her clientele at the early age of nine. Through faith in God, her entrepreneurial spirit has never failed her.

A former model, Gwendolyn has been a hair stylist most of her life. Determined to be an example of God-fearing obedience to young women, Mama Gwen shares wisdom and encouragement, along with the virtues of patience and forgiveness with her "angels" at every opportunity.

A testament to God's faithfulness to His children, even when they don't obey Him, Gwendolyn's first book, *Prospering Against Adversity with Patience and Forgiveness*, chronicles her life and the lessons she learned along the way. Glean wisdom from this God-fearing woman and grow in your relationship with the Lord.

Gwendolyn is currently a member of Detroit World Outreach Christian Center Church in Redford, Michigan where Bishop B.A. Gibert is senior pastor. The mother of one daughter, Gwendolyn lives in Southfield, Michigan.

To contact Mrs. Singleterry

**Mrs. Gwendolyn Singleterry**
c/o PriorityONE Publications
P.O. Box 34722
Detroit, MI 48234

info@GwendolynSingleterry.com
www.GwendolynSingleterry.com

www.ingramcontent.com/pod-product-compliance
Lightning Source LLC
Chambersburg PA
CBHW050507120526
44588CB00044B/1690